3-Chord Songs for UKULELE

ISBN 978-1-61780-372-7

HAL•LEONARD®
CORPORATION
7777 W. BLUEMOUND RD. P.O. BOX 13819 MILWAUKEE, WI 53213

Visit Hal Leonard Online at
www.halleonard.com

All Shook Up

Words and Music by Otis Blackwell and Elvis Presley

can't seem to stand _ on my own two feet. Who _____ do you thank _ when you

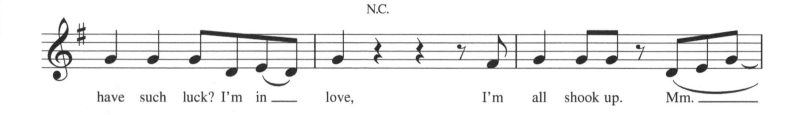

N.C.

have such luck? I'm in ___ love, I'm all shook up. Mm. _____

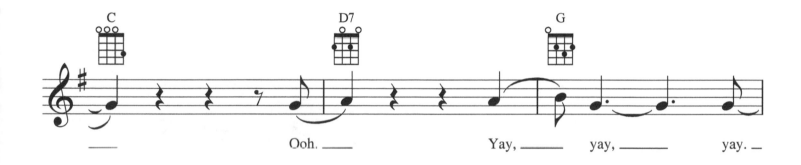

C   D7   G

_ Ooh. _ Yay, _____ yay, _____ yay. _

Verse
C

_ 3. Well-a, please __ don't ask __ me what's-a on my mind. _ I'm a

G   C

lit-tle mixed up, _ but I feel fine. _ When I'm near the girl __ that

D7   N.C.

I love best, _ my heart beats so, it scares _____ me to death. When she touched _

_____ my hand, oh, what a chill I got. Her lips are like _____ a vol -

ca - no that's hot. I'm _____ proud to say that she's my but - ter - cup. _ I'm in _

love, I'm all shook up. Mm. _____ Ooh. _

_ Yay, _____ yay, _____ yay. _____ 4. My

Verse

tongue gets tied when I try to speak. My in - sides shake _ like a

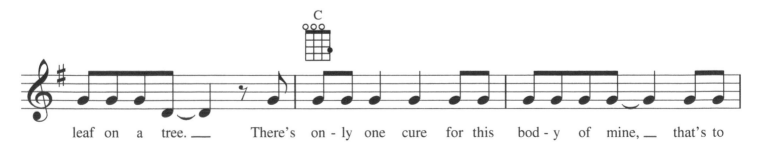

leaf on a tree. _ There's on - ly one cure for this bod - y of mine, _ that's to

have that girl and a love so fine. When she touched my hand, oh, what a

chill I got. Her lips are like a vol - ca - no that's hot. I'm

proud to say that she's my but - ter - cup. I'm in love, uh, I'm

all shook up. Mm. Ooh. Yay,

yay, yay. Ooh. Ooh.

Yay, yay. I'm all shook up.

Barbara Ann

Words and Music by Fred Fassert

Bye Bye Love

**Words and Music by Felice Bryant
and Boudleaux Bryant**

Chorus

Bye bye, love; bye bye, hap - pi - ness; _

hel - lo, lone - li - ness; _ I think I'm gon - na cry. ____

Bye bye, love; bye bye, sweet ca - ress; _

hel - lo, emp - ti - ness; _ I feel like I could die, ____ bye

1.
bye, my love, bye bye.

2.
2. I'm through with bye.

Chantilly Lace

Words and Music by J.P. Richardson

First note

Moderate Boogie Woogie

Chan - til - ly lace _____ and a pret - ty face _____

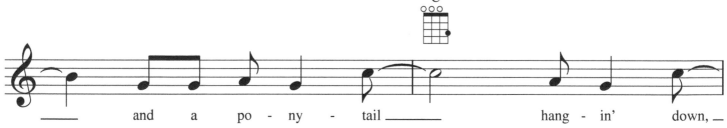

_____ and a po - ny - tail _____ hang - in' down, _____

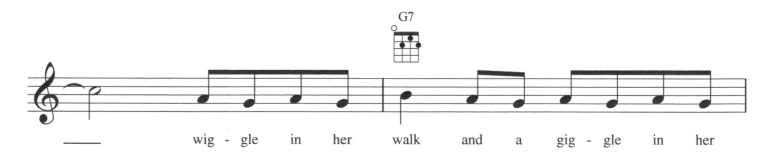

_____ wig - gle in her walk and a gig - gle in her

talk,   makes   the   world   go   'round. _____

_____ Ain't   noth - in'   in   this   world   like   a

big - eyed   girl ____ to   make   me   act   so   fun - ny,   make   me

spend   my   mon - ey,   make   me   feel   real   loose   like   a

long - necked   goose,   like   a   girl. _____

Cold, Cold Heart

Words and Music by Hank Williams

First note

Moderately

1. I tried so hard, my dear, to show that you're my ev - 'ry
(2.) nev - er know how much it hurts to see you sit and

dream. Yet you're a - fraid each thing I do is just some e - vil
cry. You know you need and want my love yet you're a - fraid to

scheme. A mem - 'ry from your lone - some past keeps us so far a -
try. Why do you run and hide from life? To try it just ain't

part. Why can't I free your doubt - ful mind and melt your cold, cold
smart. Why can't I free your doubt - ful mind and melt your cold, cold

heart? An - oth - er love be - fore my time made your heart sad and
heart? There was a time when I be - lieved that you be - longed to

blue. And so my heart is pay - ing now for things I did - n't
me. But now I know your heart is shack - led to a mem - o -

do. In an - ger, un - kind words are said that make the tear - drops
ry. The more I learn to care for you the more we drift a -

start. Why can't I free your doubt - ful mind and
part. Why can't I free your doubt - ful mind and

1.
melt your cold, cold heart? 2. You'll

2.
melt your cold, cold heart?

Do Wah Diddy Diddy

Words and Music by Jeff Barry and Ellie Greenwich

First note

Verse
Moderately

1. There he was, ___ just a - walk - in' down the street, sing - in',
(2.) fore I knew ___ it he was walk - in' next to me, sing - in',

"Do wah did - dy did - dy, down did - dy do."
"Do wah did - dy did - dy, down did - dy do." He

Pop - pin' his fin - gers and a - shuf - fl - in' his feet, sing - in',
took my hand _____ just as nat - 'ral as can be, sing - in',

"Do wah did - dy did - dy, down did - dy do." He looked
"Do wah did - dy did - dy, down did - dy do." We walked

good, (Yeah, yeah.) he looked fine. (Yeah, yeah.) He looked
on, (Yeah, yeah.) to my door. (Yeah, yeah.) We walked

good, he looked fine, and I near - ly lost my mind. 2. Be -
on to my door, and he

stayed a lit - tle more. My, my, my, my, I

knew we were fall - in' in love.

My, my, my, my, _____ I

told him all the things I was dream - in' of. _____ Now

we're to - geth - er near - ly ev - 'ry sin - gle day, sing - in',

15

"Do wah did - dy did - dy, down did - dy do."

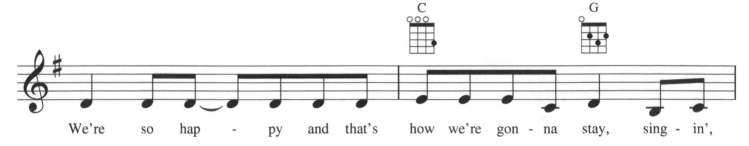

We're so hap - py and that's how we're gon - na stay, sing - in',

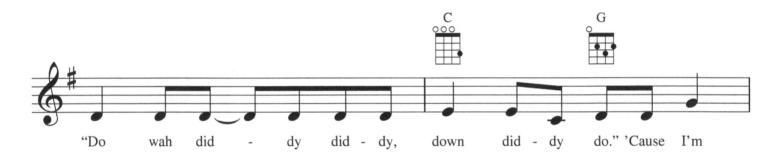

"Do wah did - dy did - dy, down did - dy do." 'Cause I'm

his, (Yeah, yeah.) and he's mine. (Yeah, yeah.) Well, I'm

his, and he's mine, and the wed - ding bells will chime, sing - in',

Repeat and fade

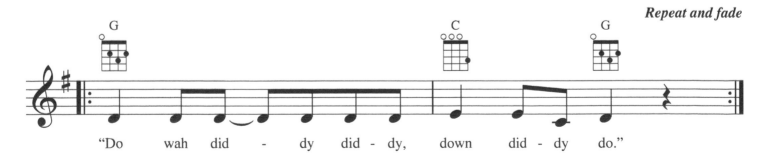

"Do wah did - dy did - dy, down did - dy do."

Elvira

Words and Music by Dallas Frazier

First note

Chorus
Moderate Country beat

El - vi - ra,   El - vi - ra,   my

heart's   on   fi - re   for El - vi - ra.

Verse

1. Eyes   that   look   like   heav - en.   Lips   like   cher - ry
(2.) night   I'm   gon - na   meet   her   at the   Hun - gry House Ca -

wine.   That   girl   can   sho'   nuff   make   my   lit - tle   light
fe,   and   I'm   gon - na   give   her   all   the   love   I

A7   **D**

shine. _____   I   get   a   fun - ny
can. _____   She's   gon - na   jump   and

G7

feel - ing   up   and   down   my   spine,
hol - ler,   'cause   I   saved   up   my   last   two   dol - lar,   and

D   **A7**   **D**

'cause   I   know   that   my   El - vi - ra's   mine. _____
we're   gon - na   search   and   find   that   preach - er   man. _____

𝄋 Chorus

D

_____   I'm   sing - in'   El - vi - ra,   El -

Get Back

Words and Music by John Lennon and Paul McCartney

1. Jo Jo was a man who thought __ he was a lon - er, but __
2. Sweet Lo - ret - ta Mar - tin thought __ she was a wom - an, but __

__ he knew it could - n't last. __ Jo __
__ she was an - oth - er man. __ All __

__ Jo left his home in Tuc - son, Ar - i - zo - na, for __
__ the girls a - round her say __ she's got it com - ing, but __

__ some Cal - i - for - nia grass. __ }
__ she gets it while she can. __ }

Get back! __

Chorus

Get back! _____ Get back _____ to where you once be - longed. _____ Get back! _ _____ Get back! _____ Get back _____ to where you once be - longed. _____ *(Get back, Jo Jo.)* _____

Hang On Sloopy

Words and Music by Wes Farrell and Bert Russell

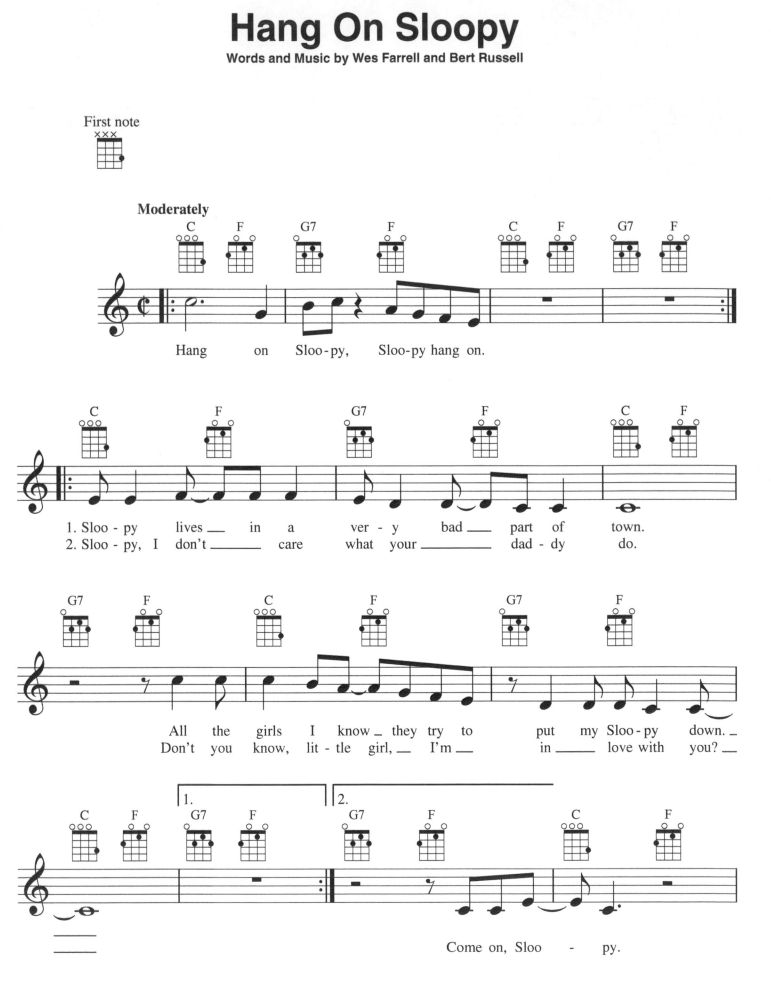

First note

Moderately

Hang on Sloo-py, Sloo-py hang on.

1. Sloo-py lives ___ in a ver-y bad ___ part of town.
2. Sloo-py, I don't _____ care what your _____ dad-dy do.

All the girls I know ___ they try to put my Sloo-py down. ___
Don't you know, lit-tle girl, ___ I'm ___ in _____ love with you? ___

1.

2.

Come on, Sloo - py.

Come on, girl. ____ Say

yeah, yeah, yeah, ____ good, good, good, good,

good, good, good, good. ____ Oh, I wan-na say

ah. ____

____ Now I want you to tell me some-thing, ba - by.

Well, don't it make you feel cra - zy? I wan-na say

ah. ____

Repeat and fade

Hang on Sloo-py, Sloo-py hang on.

23

I Fought the Law

Words and Music by Sonny Curtis

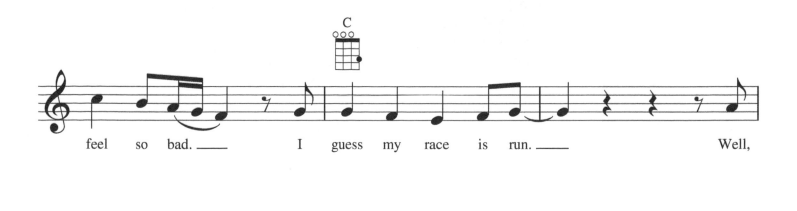

feel so bad. ____ I guess my race is run. ____ Well,

she's the best __ girl I've ev - er had. __ I fought the law __ and the

To Coda ⊕

law won. I fought the law __ and the law __

D.S. al Coda
(with repeat)

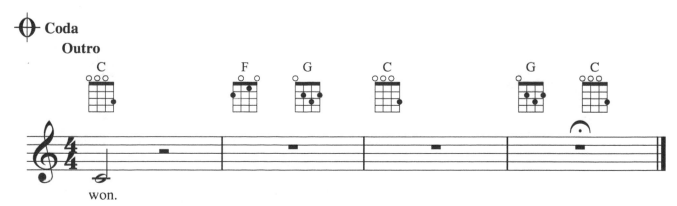

won.

3. A -

⊕ **Coda**
Outro

won.

Kansas City

Words and Music by Jerry Leiber and Mike Stoller

First note

Chorus
Bright Shuffle

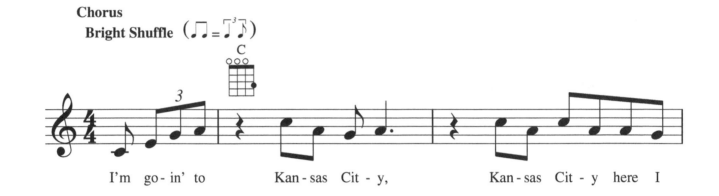

I'm go-in' to Kan-sas Cit-y, Kan-sas Cit-y here I

come. I'm go-in' to Kan-sas Cit-y,

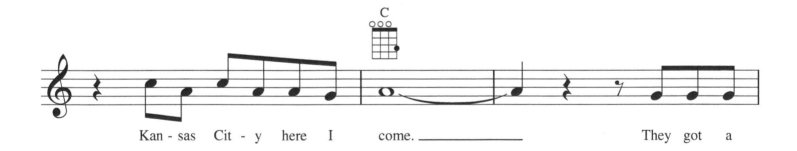

Kan-sas Cit-y here I come. They got a

cra-zy way of lov-in' there and I'm gon-na get me some.

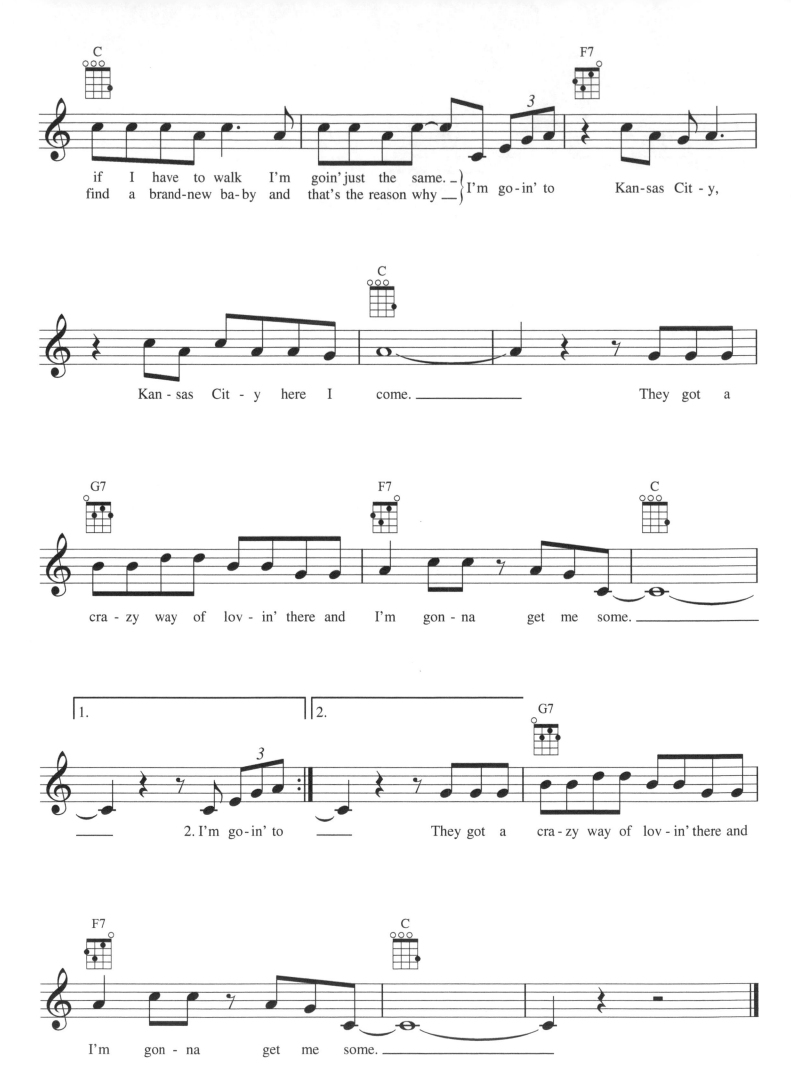

if I have to walk I'm goin' just the same. _ I'm go-in' to Kan-sas Cit - y,
find a brand-new ba-by and that's the reason why _

Kan - sas Cit - y here I come. _____ They got a

cra - zy way of lov - in' there and I'm gon - na get me some. _____

1.
_____ 2. I'm go-in' to

2.
_____ They got a cra - zy way of lov - in' there and

I'm gon - na get me some. _____

Lay Down Sally

**Words and Music by Eric Clapton,
Marcy Levy and George Terry**

First note

Verse
Brightly

1. There is noth - ing that ____ is wrong ___ in
(2.) sun ain't near - ly on ____ the rise, ___ and
(3.) long to see ___ the morn - ing light ___

want - ing you ___ to stay ____ here ___ with me.
we still got ___ the moon and stars ___ a - bove.
col - or - ing ___ your face so dream - i - ly.

I know you've got ___ some - where ___ to go, ___ but
Un - der - neath ___ the vel - vet skies, ___
So don't you go ___ and say ____ good - bye; ___

won't you make your - self at home and stay with me?

love is all that mat - ters. Won't you stay with me?

you can lay your wor - ries down and stay with me.

And don't you ev - er leave.

And don't you ev - er leave.

And don't you ev - er leave.

Chorus

Lay down, Sal - ly, and rest you in my arms.

Don't you think you want some - one to talk

to?

Lay down, Sal -

- ly;   no   need   to   leave __ so   soon. ____

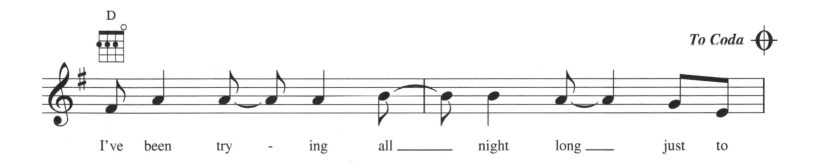

I've   been   try   -   ing   all _____ night   long ____   just   to

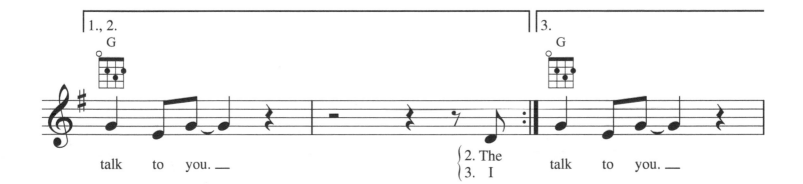

talk   to   you. ____   { 2. The   talk   to   you. ____
                                          { 3. I

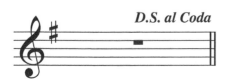

D.S. al Coda

Coda

talk   to   you. ____

La Bamba

By Ritchie Valens

Love Me Do

**Words and Music by John Lennon
and Paul McCartney**

First note

Chorus
Moderate Shuffle

Love, love me do, ___ you know I love you.

___ I'll al - ways be true. ___ So please, ___

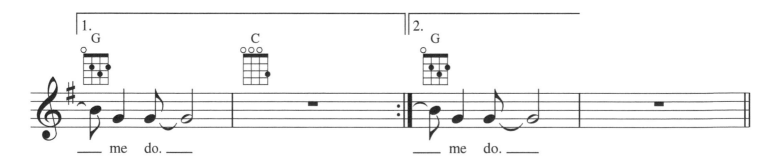

love me do. ___ Whoa. ___ Love ___

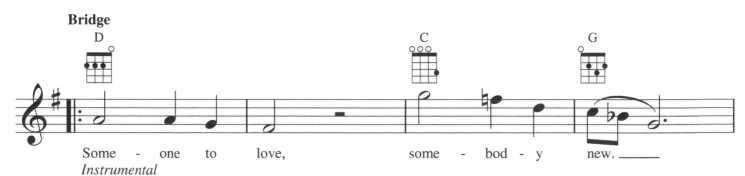

1. ___ me do. ___ 2. ___ me do. ___

Bridge

Some - one to love, some - bod - y new. ___
Instrumental

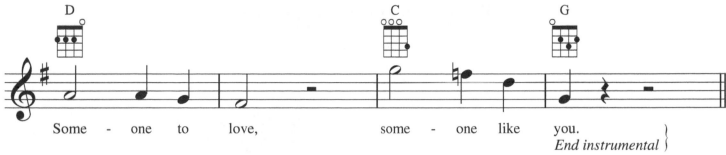

Some - one to love, some - one like you.

End instrumental

Chorus

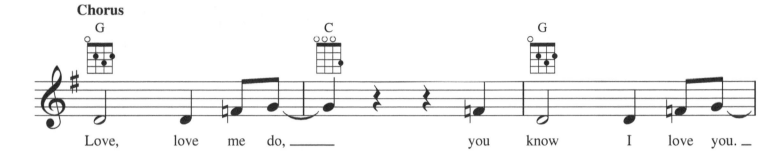

Love, love me do, _____ you know I love you. _

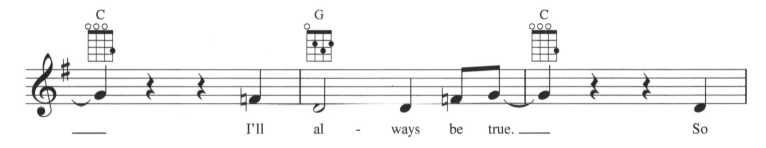

_ I'll al - ways be true. _____ So

N.C.

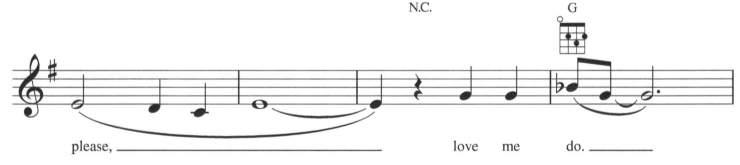

please, _____ love me do. _____

1.

Whoa. _____ Love _____ me do. _____

2.

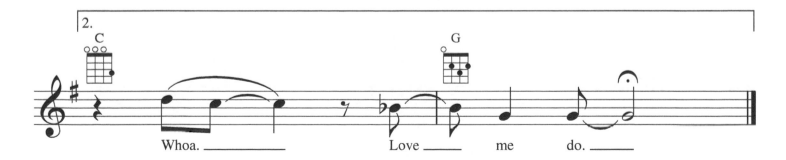

Whoa. _____ Love _____ me do. _____

Mellow Yellow

Words and Music by Donovan Leitch

1. I'm just mad a-bout Saf - fron, _____ Saf-fron's mad a-bout me. _____
2. I'm just mad a-bout Four - teen, _____ Four-teen's mad a-bout me. _____
3. Born high for-ev-er to _____ fly, _____ wind ve-loc-i-ty: nill. _____
4. *Instrumental*

I'm - a just mad a-bout Saf - fron, _____
I'm - a just mad a-bout Four - teen, _____
Born _ high for-ev-er to _____ fly, _____

she's just mad a-bout me. _____
she's just mad a-bout me. _____
if you want your cup I will fill. _____

They call me Mel-low Yel-low. _____ *(Spoken:) Quite rightly.*

(4.)*(Instrumental continues)*

They call me Mel-low Yel-low. _____ *Quite rightly.* They call me Mel-low

Yel - low. _____
(4.) *(End instrumental)*

To Coda (last time)

1., 2., 4.

Stir It Up

Words and Music by Bob Marley

First note

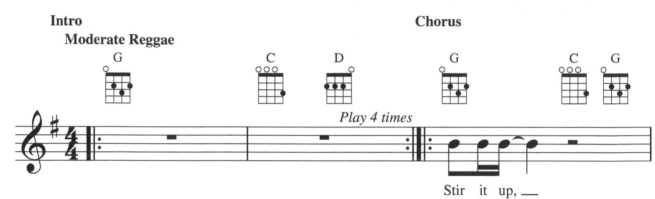

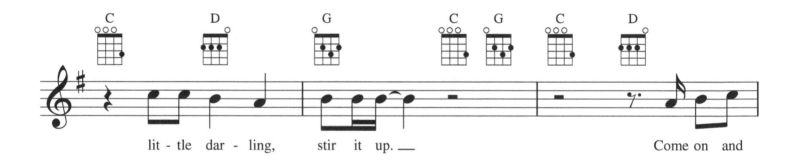

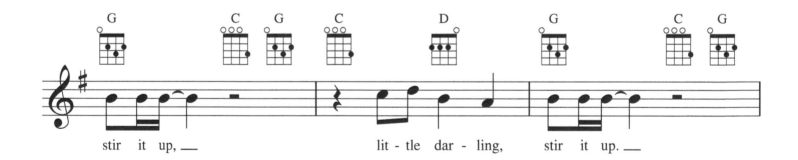

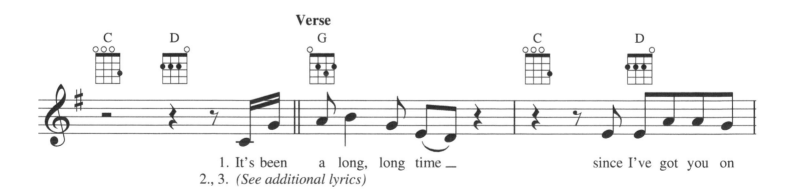

Additional Lyrics

2. I'll push the wood, I'll blaze your fire,
   Then I'll satisfy your, your heart's desire.
   Said I'll stir it, yeah, ev'ry minute, yeah.
   All you got to do, honey, is keep it in.

3. Oh, will you quench me while I'm thirsty?
   Or would you cool me down when I'm hot?
   Your recipe, darling, is so tasty,
   And you sure can stir your pot.

Surfin' U.S.A.

Words and Music by Chuck Berry

surf - in' U. S. A. _____
surf - in' U. S. A. _____

2. You'll catch 'em surf - in' at
4. At Hag - ger - ty's ___ and

Verse

Del Mar, ___
Swa - mi's, ___

Ven - tu - ra Coun - ty Line, _____
Pa - cif - ic Pal - i - sades, _____

_____ San - ta Cruz and Tres - tles, ___
_____ San O - no - fre and Sun - set, ___

Aus - tra - lia's Nar - ra - been. _
Re - don - do Beach, L. A. _____

_____ All o - ver Man - hat - tan _____
_____ All o - ver La Jol - la, _____

and down Do - he - ny Way, ___
at Wa - i - me - a Bay, ___

ev - 'ry - bod - y's gone surf - in', _____
ev - 'ry - bod - y's gone surf - in', _____

1.
_____ surf - in' U. S. A. _____

3. We'll all be plan - nin' out a

2.
_____ surf - in' U. S. A. _____

41

Tutti Frutti

Words and Music by Little Richard Penniman
and Dorothy La Bostrie

Additional Lyrics

2. I got a gal, her name's Daisy,
   She almost drives me crazy.
   I got a gal, her name's Daisy,
   She almost drives me crazy.
   She's a real gone cookie, yes sir-ee,
   But pretty little Suzy's the gal for me.

Willie and the Hand Jive

Words and Music by Johnny Otis

1. I know a cat named Way - Out Wil - lie.
2. Pa - pa told Wil - lie, "You'll ru - in my home. __
3. Ma - ma, ma - ma, look at Un - cle Joe. __
4. Doc - tor and a law - yer and an In - dian chief. __
5. Wil - lie and Mil - lie got mar - ried last fall. __

He got a cool lit - tle chick called Rock - in' Mil - lie.
You and that Hand - Jive has got to go." __
He's do - in' the Hand - Jive with sis - ter Flo. __
Now they all dig that cra - zy beat. __
They had a lit - tle Wil - lie jun - ior and that ain't all. __

He can walk and stroll and
Wil - lie said, "Pa - pa don't
Grand - ma gave ba - by
Way - Out Wil - lie gave 'em
Well, the ba - by got fa - mous in his

Su - sie Q. ____ And
put me down. __ They're
sis - ter a dime. __ Said,
all a treat. __ When he
crib, you see. ____

G

do that cra - zy Hand - Jive too. ____
do - in' the Hand Jive all o - ver town." __
"Do that Hand - Jive one more time." __
did that Hand - Jive with his feet. __
Do - in' the Hand - Jive on T - V. ____

C7   G

Hand - Jive.   Hand - Jive.

D7   C7

Hand - Jive.   Do - in' that cra - zy Hand -

1.– 4.   5.
G   G

Jive.   5. Now,   Jive. _____

Mony, Mony

Words and Music by Bobby Bloom, Tommy James,
Ritchie Cordell and Bo Gentry